Ida Patton

Always be blessed

How About a Little Love

Poetry

by

C.W. Papin

Copyright © 2007 C. W. Papin

All rights reserved. No part of this book may be reproduced in any form or by any means, electronic or mechanical, including photo-copying, recording, or by any information storage and retrieval system, without written permission from the author. This excludes a reviewer who may quote brief passages in a review. For additional information, please contact the author at cpapin0905@aol.com

Cover Design:

ISBN 13: 978-0-9814650-3-6
ISBN 10: 0-9814650-3-X

Published by G Publishing, LLC
P. O. Box 24374
Detroit, MI 48224

Library of Congress Control Number: 2008922431

Printed in the United States of America

Acknowledgments

It is often said that poetry is the main residence of the language of love. However, it is also home to philosophical discourse and commentary about the societal conditions that surround all of us.

The collection of poems, contained in the pages of this book, visit many of the dwellings that house stories about the social condition and situations that make life what it is today. The manner in which the material in this book is presented is the result of the encounters and inspiration of countless people that have shared my life's journey. Some of the travelers, like my parents, shared many miles of my journey, and guided me toward a spot in time where I could make a meaningful contribution. Others shared varying numbers of steps along my path. All of them in some way or other helped to shape and influence the views of the world portrayed in this work.

It is not possible to individually thank all of the people who have helped to make this book possible, but several people have done their best to keep me motivated and encouraged. These include Joe Baker, who would call and ask how the project was coming. Dr. Fleming kept telling me to publish my work. A special thank you goes to Storyteller and Poet Gerald McLamore, who gave me the opportunity to present my work to our Fellowship Chapel family during each years' African Queen's Day celebration. The elegant cover design was created by Gwen Gipson

Thank you seems to be an inadequate expression of gratitude when applied to my wife, Shirley, who in addition to her constant encouragement, was my chief editor and proofreader.

This book is dedicated to my Father, Hydle Papin and to the memory of my Mother, Marion V. Papin

TABLE OF CONTENTS

SECTION I Miscellaneous Musings
    Dis an Dat   11
    First Light   12
    How About a Little Love   13
    The Persuader   15
    Guns   17
    The Choir   19
    Another Day   21
SECTION II Family Matters
    Matrimonial Lament   25
    A Whisper to a Scream   27
    Grandparents Joy   30
    Welcome Home   32
    All These Years   34
    It's Time   36
    Don't Shed No Tears   38
SECTION III America Today
    Let Me Make it Very Clear   43
    Stormy Weather   45
    Somebody Please Set Me Free   47
    Terrorists in the Land   49
    Unwinding A Twisted Perception   51
SECTION IV African Queens
    Queens Day   57
    Lost Queens   59
    Wear Your Crown Right   61
    Go Fetch – if You're Ready   63

SECTION V Seasons and Special Days

Winter's Landfall	67
A Special Day	68
Graduation Day	69
The Race	70
A Turkey's Tale	71
Christmas Morn	72
A Sailor's Winter	73

MISCELLANEOUS MUSINGS

In this section are pieces about this, and pieces about that, including one called Dis and Dat. Something in this section just might touch, tickle, or appeal to your conscious reflections about the world that surrounds us.

Dis an Dat

Did you get the word I sent out?
Wrote a few lines bout dis an dat
Thought bout my sistahs,
Bout my brodda too.
Had to write fast
Afor my thoughts sho nuff flew
Things from my heart
All of them true.

Wrote a little bit of dis an dat bout motha
She sho was good,
I knows God is resting her soul
Thinking bout her
I can't help gettin carried away.

Wrote a line bout dad
Then stopped to pray
Lord befoe I'm done,
Don't let my words fade away.

Wrote a little dis bout my she chile
And wrote a bit of dat bout my he chile
But, about my husband,
I wrote a little dis an dat.

Now that I've started,
I can't let the doubts of my head
Stifle the creativity
Coming from my heart

For Sister

First Light

First Light, is like the embers of a dying bon fire illuminating the ground, appearing like tiny streaks of yellow paint dashed upon the leaves of a tree.

First Light, is the prelude to a new day bathed in the promises of fulfilling untold dreams. Dreams that cannot be extinguished by the darkness of night.

First Light is like new lovers, with a spiders web of silk, gently wrapped around them that is as fragile as the unseen bonds of love that bind them together.

First Light is like the cry of a newborn child, announcing the start of a new life that is yet to be challenged by the cares of this world.

First Light is like the lifting of a veil covering an idea that is waiting to climb out of the recesses of one's mind, ready to join the vast body of knowledge that delineates life's journey.

First Light, brings with it the promise of a fresh new chance to change the disappointments and failures of yesterday into the successes of today.

What would a day be without the magnificence of First Light peaking over the mountains, creeping down the walls of the valleys, and projecting a shimmering reflective glow across the seas? Thank God for First Light.

How about a Little Love

Need I be angry, loud, and profane
Before as a poet
You know my name.
Must everyone's work
Sound just the same?
Is talk of love
Just a little too tame?
Can love instead of self-hate
Bring about change?

While white men
Should shoulder the bulk of the blame.
Only we can change our condition
After 400 years of shame.
Rip that dope monkey off your back.
Get rid of that pipe
Stop smoking crack.
Rebound from the fall,
And take your life back!

Stop carrying that gun
Everywhere you go.
Do you really need a piece
In a picture show?
Stop killing brothers
You don't even know.

If you can't love others,
You don't even know by name.
Then nothing we do
Will ever bring about change.
Do you get the message
Or need I be profane?

The Persuader

The persuader I knew
Was not what you might think.
It was not a profound man,
Or a notable book.
It was a black razor strap
Hanging on a hook.

Two feet long
And three inches wide
Handled with deft skill
It was very effective
When repeatedly applied to my hide.

There were chores to be done,
And rules to be obeyed.
If you stepped out of line
It was with the persuader
That you'd spend some time.

Dinner was at five and when I was late.
I was told to get the persuader
Then go upstairs and wait.
I'd be dealt with
After Dad cleaned his plate.

He said what he meant
And he meant what he said.
Now the persuader would do
The rest of the talking that day.

Pull down those pants
Your backside is mine
Thump, thump, thump
On my rump, rump, rump
That's the way the persuader spoke.

Its been years since my behind
Has been in such a painful bind.
But if a whipping was what it took
To make me the man that I am today?
Then thanks to the Persuader
Is all I have to say.

Guns

Guns are everywhere
Guns for everyone
Short ones
Long ones
Big ones
Small one
Got One?
Get one!

Guns, Guns, Guns!
There's enough for everyone
They can kill anyone.

Guns, Guns, Guns!
We want them
We need them
We Love them
I hate them!

Guns, Guns, Guns!
Take them everywhere
To the store
In the car
To the Bar
Off to school
You fool!

Guns, Guns, Guns!
Mindless pieces of steel
Imposing brainless people's will
Killing folks for a thrill
This scourge across our land
Is completely out of hand

Guns, Guns, Guns!
I often wonder
How one could love a Gun
When all it does
Is kill, wound, and maim
Are these people heart-less
Or just insane?

It would be fine with me
If I never saw a Gun again!

The Choir

Somewhere between the prayer
And the preaching
There was singing by the choir
Whose spirit filled voices
Set the congregation on fire.

For many years
As I sat in the pews
The thought formostin my head,
That singing in the choir
Was my heart's true desire.

I built up my courage
And off to rehearsal I went
Hoping the Choir Director would think
That my voice was heaven sent.

It was without an audition
That I became a member of the choir,
Fulfilling one of my life's ambitions.

Rehearsals, sometimes fun,
Sometimes long, are sometimes rough.
The Director is always tough
As he strives
To get the best out of us.

In frustration he sighs
And then he shouts,
"You won't leave this room
Until you sing this song in tune."

All of the practicing is done

And our prayer has begun
"Join our souls together,
Make our spirits as one.
Let our music praise
The One on high
And move the peoples spirits
Up into a heavenly sky."

Its Sunday morning,
And we're forty strong.
There's a heavenly refrain
To all of our songs.

The Spirit of the Lord
So alive in the choir
Is evident in every chord,
As with uplifted voices,
We sing praises to the Lord

The people cry, jump up,
Clap, and shout.
But even as we sway, rock, and sing
that's not what the choir's mission
Is really about.

If, while singing our songs,
The choir heals someone's wounded soul,
Or helps another
Make his shattered life whole
The mission of the choir
Has been fulfilled.

Another Day

Awakened by a shaft of light in my room
Shot like an arrow
From the morning sun.
Dust particles dance in the light.
Another day beacons
There's much work to be done.

My head lifts slowly from the pillow
I climb gingerly out of bed
The pain that I feel
As my feet touch the floor.
Is very real and not just in my head.

I get on the road
In the warmth of a sun.
Pulled into the sky
By a force unseen.
So many errands yet to be run
I hurry along as fast I can

With steps that are painful and slow.
I try to keep moving along
As the day moves along, I stop for a rest
Getting relief from the heat of the sun
Got to get moving I'm too old to run
My journey is just about done.

The shadows have now grown long
Casting designs upon the walls.
The dark overcoming the light
Signals the end of another day.
I smile in spite of the pain.

Its time to seek the comfort of sleep
I need some relief from my mental strain.
I pray not, but tomorrow may bring
More of the same.

With the love of the Lord
In my heart
A prayer of thanksgiving
On my lips
A feeling of contentment
In my soul
I slip off to sleep.

Knowing that all to soon
It will again be ANOTHER DAY.

Family Matters

Under attack from every direction, the family is still the foundation of our lives. Comprised of tragedy, trials, tribulations, and triumphs, the family is the web that binds us to one another. The family is our fountain of love. Its waters fall on the loving, the contrary, the functional, and the dysfunctional members that make up every family. Love is the essence of family.

Matrimonial Lament

There once was a time
Some many years ago.
That when a babe
Was but a teeny bundle of joy.
An unwed mother's father
With shotgun in hand
Would escort the baby's father
To the preacher and say
"You have a choice on this blessed day
To marry or in the ground
You will surely lay."

But that was then and this is now
We get the milk
Without buying the cow.
No need for a ceremony
Or the exchange of gold rings

Where is the love for each other
When the "Now Generation"
Has meaningless sex at thirteen?

Where is the love for the children
When young girls
Become mothers at fourteen?

Fathers, jailed or dead by eighteen.
The thought of family
Has been wiped away clean.

But lets not forget
It's not just the teens
That makes "Single-Parent Homes"
Reign supreme.

Is it that fateful trip to the alter
That makes young people's steps falter.
Without marriage as a driving force
There's no worry about
The prospect of divorce.

If it's not love that you seek
Or love that you have
If you can't take the plunge
And the step into marriage is too tall.
It's better by far
Not to have any children at all.

A Whisper to a Scream

Used to be, that I need not speak
You could sense my moods
Without a peep.
We were young and love was fresh
Our minds and spirits
Would magically mesh.

Did you hear me, I heard her say
"Yes, yes, yes
For the third time today."

No matter what I do or say
Getting your attention takes all day.
I still have needs that only you can fulfill,
But instead of your attention,
I get the big chill.

Did you hear that, I heard her say.
"Yes, heavens yes,
For the fourth time today."

Now that the children are grown and gone
Why is there so little love
Between dusk and dawn?
Is it because I've gained a few pounds
And my figure is just
A wee bit more round?
Are you still happy that
I'm the one you found?

Did you hear me,
Do I have to shout, I heard her say.
"Yes, yes, hell yes,
For the fifth time today."

Turn off that TV
And look me in the face.
The way you ignore and treat me
Is a downright disgrace.
Its time for a change
Or you might have to leave this place
Do I have your attention,
My sweet, my love.
Hear me now
Or you might need help from above.
Don't you still love me
After year thirty-three?

I looked up and said,
"Are you talking to me?"

"Why are you so loud?
What's the fuss?
You've raised enough hell for both of us.
I've stuck by your side
Through the good times and the bad.
So, why all the confusion?
Have you just gone mad?"

"I've tried to provide
All the things you held dear,
And now you threaten
To put me out of here!
Stop your talking and listen to me.
Lets make this scene
Abundantly clear."

"Can't say that I still hear your whisper.
Perhaps our minds and spirits
No longer magically mesh.
That doesn't mean
That I love you any less."

"It might require some sweetness
In your voice,
To elevate the volume
Of your words in my ears.
You can change that scream
To a mellow refrain."

I suppose I was a little sharp
And a hug and a kiss
Would be a good start.

"Yes, yes, yes, for the first time today,
I can hear you again."

Grandparents Joy

He came into our home
Disguised as a bundle of joy.
We should have known
Before his cover was blown,
That lurking in that blanket
Was a mischievous,
Soon to be rambunctious boy

At first, he was sweet and a joy
Drinking his milk and falling asleep
That scene did not prepare us
 For what was ahead.

It's dawn, as I lay asleep in my bed.
When without warning
A stealthy figure grabs at my head.
He pulls back the covers
And pinches my nose
Sitting on my chest
Just inches from my face
He whispers in my ear
"Grandpa, grandpa, get out of bed"!

Running around the house
He screams and shouts.
A darting little figure
That won't come when you call.
Stopping for a minute
He draws on the wall.
Some days that boy
Just won't mind at all!

Just as you're getting
To the end of your rope
He climbs into your lap.
Giving you a hug, he takes a nap.

In spite of the havoc
He creates each day.
What a great time we have watching
Our grandson at play.

That thinly disguised
Mischievous,
Rambunctious
Little boy.
Is indeed
Still a wonderful bundle of joy.

Welcome Home

In a ritual played out across the land
Grown children going away
To start a new home,
Has always been a part of God's grand plan.
With great fanfare, they walk out the door
Glory, halleluiah,
They don't live here any more.

Now don't take it wrong
Because I'm smiling and singing a song.
I still love my children dearly
And, there's nothing wrong
With one visit yearly.
But thanks to God,
They're gone, gone, gone.

It seemed like we were in heaven
Just the miss's and me.
I could take naps and relax
Stretched out on the couch
There was no reason
For me to argue and be a grouch.

Suddenly, there was a fateful knock
On the door.
It marked the end of peace in our home.
And the start of an unending war.

In they rumbled, son, wife,
And two unruly kids.
If they've come here to stay
I'll probably blow my lid.
I thought the message was very clear

We only wanted one visit per year.
Six months have come and gone.
Dear God, where did we go wrong?
I didn't mind if they came for a day
But why, oh why did they have to stay.

The house is now in shambles
With the kids running amok.
I've been kicked in the leg
And punched in the gut.
Comfy in bed each day they sleep late,
While finding a job is definitely
Not on their plate.

When I reminisce about our lost golden years
I just fall down in a fit of tears.
It's some comfort to know
That we're not alone.
This is a plight being felt across the land.
Life is tough and we must lend a hand.
Just pray for strength, and do what you can.

All These Years

Me, a Great, Great Grandpa
It's my day to celebrate, but wait!
Why celebrate?
What's to celebrate?
What's all the fuss about, anyhow?

No doubt, I've lived a day or two.
But that won't get you in who's who
Day by day, I've encountered every obstacle
Didn't name em,
But I surely overcame them.

A father I've been
For sixty-one years.
And, that's been good
For a whole lot of tears.
Thirty-five years a Grand Father,
I can claim.
Me, a Great, Great Grandpa,
Was that really my aim!

Worked for years,
Through rain and shine
Been retired for quite a long time
Played many a hand of cards you know,
And in Grand Masters style,
Its been a real show

I've left a legacy of self-sufficient offspring.
Been a husband for more years
Than one can count.
Now that's something
To crow about.

Time well spent,
These eighty-five years. Wait!
Did I say eighty –five years?
Its time, I think, to sit down
And have a drink.

It's Time

It seems so strange
That after all this time
No ties been found that binds to me,
A son that's mine.
Nothings been seen, felt, or found
Signals sent out across the land
Returned again and again without a sign
That this son knows that he is surely mine.

No need for DNA
Or a scholarly dissertation
A glance in a mirror,
Just look at his face.
Maybe a look at his walk
So much frustration,
Let's have a little talk.

It seems so strange
That after all this time,
With the holidays just past
Not a note or a word of greeting
Just to wish me well.
Can it be that he is unconscious
Or under a spell?
Either way the condition is temporary
And surely won't last.

It seems so strange
That after all this time,
He seems to be hung up
On the could-a-be's
Should-a-be's,
Would-a-be's,
And Want-a-be's

Nothing can change
That which was,
Like we can change
That which will be

It seems so strange
That after all this time,
He hasn't figured out
That his being mad
Does not translate
Into me being sad.
Relationships are mutually created
Requiring attention from one's mind
Tempered with input from the heart

Between you and I
It's a good place to start

Don't Shed No Tears

Been so long since I been born
Don't shed no tears for all them years
They never bad, just some better than others
Got me some aches and pains
Didn't have before
Got to be important
Before I walk out the door
My back is bent, but my spirit's upright
I've traveled life's journey and won the fight

Still got me some kin folks
Ain't none of them close at hand
Seem like they spread out
All over the land
But I've got me a phone
And they comes when I call
When they show up,
We'll have a ball
No need for me
To feel lonely at all

Most of my friends now are all gone
Same as my memories that have faded
They marched lockstep,
Disappearing in a fog
Now don't get me wrong,
I miss everyone
But life's been too good for me to be sad
Ain't going to give back a day that I've had

Throughout this sometime bumpy ride
My wife was always at my side
Guiding my path with a gentle touch
Holding me back
When I've said too much
The stars have risen up in the night
But the sun still lights the days in my life
Don't shed no tears for all them years

AMERICA TODAY

Conditions and ideologies, contributing to the reduction in the quality of life of some, and the enduring lack of improvements in the quality of life for countless others, are reflected in the poetry found in this section.

Let Me Make it Very Clear

2008 is a Presidential election year
And the battle lines have been drawn
Much idiotic rhetoric is already in high gear.
Has one of the candidates gotten your ear?

Stop, take a breath, and back up a bit
Think about how much money
Will be spent
To get a job
That pays little more than the rent.
And who it is,
That will reap the benefit.

Five hundred million bucks
Give or take a few,
Is enough money to obscure
Any President's view.

No need to worry about
Where the money came from
The candidates have promised
To look out after everyone.

The winner can be a Black man,
White man, or Woman,
It doesn't really matter who.
After spending these huge sums of money
Will they care about me and you?

When inaugurated
To the sounds of loud cheers
Who is it that will have the President's ear?
Do you think that it will be you and me
That he'll hear?

Somehow, I think not!

Stormy Weather

Terrified by the storm's great size
And how the wind howled and blew.
Middle-class folk mounted their SUV's
And up the byways they flew.

The evacuation ordered
For citizens in town.
Meant nothing to poor folk
Without the means to get around.

As the flood waters in the city rose
The brains of bureaucrats suddenly froze.
The President stayed far away from the fray.
Hoping that FEMA would save the day.

A decision had to be made before the night.
Shall we rescue some Negroes
Before first light,
Or let them die and sink out of sight?
The corpses of black folk left to die
Left our people wondering
Why, oh God, why!

This once great city is now a sea of mud.
Filled with houses torn apart
By the mighty flood.
The people's wait for help was in vain
As the efforts of FMEA failed with a thud.
Displaced people spread out all across the land
blessed by folks who lent them a hand.

Since the time of the storm

Many months have come and gone.
Unfulfilled plans of rebirth are still the norm.
Most of the rebuilding is yet undone.

All is not lost,
As inspired people build by day.
All is not right,
As "Brooks Brothers" clad thieves
Work thru the night, figuring ways
To steal poor folks property rights.
Taking back our city will take a
Long, long, hard fight!

When New Orleans rises from the dust
Will any of it still belong to us?
If things continue like they seem
Cheap housing around the Quarter
Will only exist in our dreams.

Unlike the sad lyrics of a bluesy song
We'll not be packing up and moving along.
This city has always been our home.
This is where we'll always be.
It's where we rightfully belong!

Somebody Please Set Me Free

I was told by informed sources
That for ages I've been free.
So won't somebody please
Get these shackles off of me.

Everyone could plainly see
I was on my way to the top.
Surrounded by fine things
In my house by the sea.
So why did the feel of the ghetto
Still abide in me?

I went to work
In a three-piece suit
And I made plenty of loot.
But, at the hint of a promotion
The office became an arena of commotion.

Was something amiss in my work?
Was there a quirk in the way I look?
I reached the sobering conclusion.
That my freedom was only a cruel illusion.

At the first business downturn
I was the first to get the boot.
So off, to many interviews, I went
Where I got the same old look.
They smiled while glancing at my resume
Then without fanfare
They politely gave me the hook.

When they said I was free
Were they just being nice to me?

I'm in the unemployment line at one.
All my bills and the mortgage are past due.
I feel helpless and in so much pain
But it's my wife and children being stung.

My fairytale world has become undone.
So, tell me again about being free
Then show me how that state of being
Applies to me!

Yes, I know
That your life has been tough.
And by now you have had
Quite enough.
The shackles that you feel,
But cannot see
Can only be opened by you
Without any help from me.

Open your eyes
To see the new light.
Activate your mind
To remove your fright
Muster courage
To continue the fight

Then pray, pray, pray, pray
That everything
Will turn out all right.

Terrorists in Our Land

911, the day great buildings
Fell to the ground.
Thousands killed instantly
In a horrific flash
Prompting the government
To dole out to its victims
Millions in cash.

Was a lapse in security
The government's fault
Causing them to tap Fort Knox's great vault?
So why doesn't this benevolence extend to us.

Does a terrorist only attack
By flying a plane?
Or can he drive a car
To where we are?

A child without a care in the world
Walking to a neighborhood store
Cut down by gunfire from a drive-by.
Life in her body is no more.

Was this drive-by killing a terrorist attack?
Will the government send out some cash?
Or is there some element
That this attack lacked?

Do the government manuals say
That a terrorist must be an Arab man
Armed with a homemade suicide bomb
Cast as a member of some radical
Islamic band?

Or can he be an inner-city thug
With an automatic pistol in his hand
Creating havoc, by dealing dope,
In ghettos across this land?

Are the assaults, faced by people every day,
And the killings and muggings
Where our children play
Unimportant to a government
Sensitive only to power and wealth.

Must poor people be satisfied
With the hand they've been dealt?
Or is Uncle Sam ready
To provide us with a little help?
I don't recommend
That you hold your breath
Just suck it up and tighten your belt.

Help is not on the way.

Unwinding A Twisted Perception

I live in an Urban Center
That's the Ghetto to you.

You know!
The place that you fear
And don't want to come near.

You hear!
Daily stories in the news
That feed your twisted views

Stories about!
Drug dealers, crime, and death
Bungling at city hall
Politicians headed for a fall
Public school students
Learning little or not at all
Unwed mothers in welfare lines
Young boys busted
And doing time.

Pictures of!
Crime scenes and victims
Buildings boarded up
Houses burned down
Helpless, hungry, homeless
Hopeless people all around

While we!
Read it in the paper
And see it on TV
It is disheartening and sad
That this message of self-hate
Too often, comes from us.

Makes us!
Believe that the place of our birth,
Is the worst place on earth.

Are we?
A collection of worthless blots
Smudged across life's landscape
A drab collogue
Of lost, hopeless souls.

The Ghetto!
In this discouraging mirage,
Is part real and part false.
Now is the time for this portrait
Of Ghetto life, crime, and strife
To be repainted and made right.

We will!
Need an end to black folks collusion
To rebuke these cruel illusions

I see!
The enemy,
And it is us!
We are the ones that preach
That unless you're poor
You can't live here any more
We won't even shop
At a neighborhood store.

We must!
Eliminate the notion
That the measure of our success
Is how far we can get
From the place that we're from.

We can!
Stop advancing the notion
That the Ghetto
Is home only for;
Bad Folks, Black Folks
Crazy Folks, Crooked Folks
Shiftless, Sorry Ass' Folks
Poor Folks,
And my Folks.

We know!
That life in the Ghetto
Is more than this false story
It's time for us, without hesitation,
To teach our people the truth
About this twisted perception

This is!
The Ghetto that I know
It's home to;
Church folks, Caring Folks
Black Folks, Family Folks,
Hard working Folks
Good Folks, My Folks,
And your Folks

We need!
To teach our children
That it is a lie
That the worst place on earth
Is the place of their birth.
Tell the children
That this is their land
Tell them to say it loud
This is my home
And I'm blessed and I'm proud.

African Queens

The pieces found in this section are dedicated to the Mothers, Daughters, Wives, Grandmothers, Big Mamas, and Sisters in American, who are of African decent.

African American women have been thrust into the role of "Head of Household", by a system of oppression that had its roots in slavery. Today the absence of men as the "Head of Household", in the Black Community is being perpetuated by the cloud of racial injustice under which we live.

In spite of their burdens, these Ebony Goddesses surround us with their warmth, make a place for us with their intelligence, support us with their strength, beguile us with their beauty, and comfort us with their love.

Queens Day

Today is your ay my African Queens
A thoughtful set aside
But let's not forget,
This is all you get!
So, before you arise
Like a bee from her hive
I'll tell you some good stuff
So I can leave this place alive.

African Queens,
This being your day
You have been put duly in charge.
Aggravation from men folks
Has been put on hold.
We know you're always right
Without ever being told
At your command,
We will not question why.
With no hesitation
We'll leap for the sky

The honey due list has been scrutinized
The legions of items prioritized.
The children have been fed
And the dog has been walked.
Thank goodness dinner
Has already been cooked.

African Queens, on this special day
We want you to know
That we love you all
And in the spirit of this day
The third and fourth lines of this poem
Are subject to recall.

LOST QUEEN

She has ruled for eons.
Was it from a jeweled throne?
A tower of strength,
This ebony Queen
So how is it that she is still unseen?

Black men blinded
By a culture cruel and cold.
Searching for their African Queen
In a palace made of Gold.

Where is that woman in a silken gown?
Her head adorned with a Golden Crown
So beautiful, so wise, so strong, so kind.
She's nowhere to be found.

But, oh my brother,
Have you looked in the kitchen today?
Have you looked at that woman beside you,
As in your bed you lay?
Who is it, taking care of the children
Day by day.
Did you see that beautiful woman
On her way to work?
That angel of mercy
That soothed your pain.
Finding time each day
To kneel down and pray.

The woman that has loved you
Thru thick and thin.
That woman that birthed you
In great pain.

That notion, my brother,
That the African Queen cannot be found
Is just in your mind.
For she has always been there
So beautiful, so wise, so strong,
So kind

Open your eyes
See your Queen!
Reach out your hand
Feel her touch!

Now rest my brothers,
For the African Queen
Rules over all the land

Wear your Crown Right

Sistah, African Queen!
Is your Crown on straight?
Don't let it fall down
To keep any kind of man around.
Sistah, check your crown.

Sistah, you who would be a Queen.
Do you look the part,
Or are you some kind of spoiled tart?
The clothes you have on,
Are tighter than tight.
All your stuff is out in plain sight!
Do you think that's what it takes
To get a man that's right?
Sistah, check your Crown!
Looks like it's
On its way down.

Are you a woman
Drawn to the beat
Like a wild animal in heat?
Does riding in fine cars
Bling, Bling Bazaars
Define who you are?
Sistah check your crown!
Looks like its
Halfway down.

When it's all been said and done
Are you the one
That ends up in just,
Any man's bed?
Sistah, check your crown!
Looks like it's
All the way down.

Sistah, its not too late
To make a date
With a change in your life.
You can start right now.
Listen up while I tell you how!

Don't be a dope
Don't do dope
Don't sleep with dopes.
Wake up, Get up, Be up!
Not high.
Demand respect
With your self-respect.
Seek the best
Because you are the best.
Stand on your courage
Don't settle for less.
Leave the mess
For all the rest.

Sistah, your Crown
Is back on your head.

GO FETCH –
IF YOU'RE READY

Hey Brother Man,
See that sister over there
She might be the African Queen for you.
Now if you want her,
You better go fetch.

But Brother Man
Before you go fetch,
I'd better give you a warning,
Cause that Sister don't want
No un-caring, Non-working,
Jive talkng, Self centered, Irresponsible,
Child making, but not Child raising,
Half steppin man

Didn't mean to put on you such a load
But, Brother Man,
If you fit the bill you might as well
Hip- hop on down the road.
But Brother Man,
If you've got a minute
I'll try to put you back in it.

Brother Man,
Are you steadfast and strong?
A Queen needs a man
That when things get tough,
Won't give up and move along.

Brother Man,
Can you curb that cussin
When you're fussin?
A Queen needs a man
Who's slow to anger.
Brother Man,
Are you sensitive and kind?
A Queen needs a man that's caring,
One not afraid of sharing.
Brother Man,
Brother Man,
Are you ready to honor and love
A women?
A Queen needs a man
On whose shoulder She can lean.

Brother Man
If you've come this far
You get the gold star.
But go fetch, not yet!

Brother Man,
Who are you and who's are you?
A Queen needs a man
That serves the one on high.

Brother Man, that women
Who could be your African Queen
Just needs man that can be a King.

Now is the time to go fetch,

If you're ready.

SEASONS & SPECIAL DAYS

Winter, Spring, Summer, Fall You can't live in Michigan without loving them all

Special days take many forms and have different meanings for each of us.. Some of these days are explored in the pieces in this section.

**"The Race," is dedicated to the 2006 crew of
KC-161 Nefertiti**

Winter's Landfall

I've sailed my ship across the seas
But now she's docked and blocked
Her sails furled, her lines curled
She's still, silent, and dark

The wind is so bitterly cold
Its touch a vicious bite
The days are growing shorter
Oh, how I wish for a little more light

Lakes are frozen solid
The rivers still with ice
Bare branches sway to and fro
Barren landscapes
Framed with snow

While the land is silent, dark and still
Rebirth is just across the hills.
In the rivers, a trickle of water appears.
Returning birds singing songs
That all can hear.

The days grow longer
As spring grows ever near.
The rivers' water will gurgle
The ice will soon disapear.
We know it's the signal
To get out our gear.

The time for sailing
Is oh so near.

A Special Day

Is this yet just another day
You know, is there something
I should say?
Are there some deeds
That need to be done?
I've scratched my brow,
So, what day is this?

Now I think I see the light.
It's about toils and burdens
Handled each day and night.
Of lullabies sung
For an infant's delight.
Sacrifices made
So that her child is all right.

Of a love, that possesses a light
That outshines the sun by day
And the stars by night.
Arms that enfold
With a protective warmth.
Must be talking about a mother or a wife
Who's made a profound difference
In a man or a child's life.

Is this yet just another day?
Absolutely not,
This is Mothers Day

Graduation Day

Like reading a good book,
A chapter is finished.
Thou you've done your best
There's still no time to rest.
Just enough time
To get ready for what's next.

A new chapter beckons
In this book called life.
Things might get a wee bit tougher
When you encounter pages
Filled with strife.
But that's just one part of life.

So, that's how it goes,
One chapter following another.
Life's building blocks,
Stacked one on top of another.
The foundation is broad
And the storyline is strong.
We see a successful ending
And seldom are we wrong.

The Race

They came from across the land.
Two hundred fifty Captains!
Three thousand eager deck hands!
A time for work and fun for everyone.

Most have come hoping to finish first.
But this crew was different, you see
They would be the first black crew
To sail in this race.

The excitement was in the air.
Spectators and sailors were everywhere.
NEFERTITI moored in the quay,
Was, with her black skipper and crew,
Ready to get underway.

Race day dawned clear and bright
We excitedly left the dock.
With a raucous shout
We cleared the start.
At the sound the gun
The adventure of a lifetime
Had finally begun. .

Feeling a fair wind in our face
A black crewed boat was in the race.
Mackinac Island was merely
Two hundred fifty miles away.

A Turkey's Tale

Thanksgiving is the time of year
That I have come to fear.
And Grandma's house
Is not at all dear.
I could lose my head
To a mighty cheer!

I've trained hard for a time like this.
They grab for my neck
And I make them miss.
I feint and I fake, I dodge and run.
The last thing I hear
Is the roar of a gun!

So here I am, basted and baked
Roasted perfectly
To somebody's taste.
Surrounded by yams, greens,
And rolls raised by yeast.
This turkey is now
The centerpiece of your feast!

Christmas Morn

Have you ever paused to wonder
While tearing wrappings
Off Christmas plunder.
How the birth of one little boy
Filled the world
With such wondrous joy!

Have you considered
While gazing at your twinkling tree.
Why the Wise Men
Numbered not one, or two, but three?
And while possibly rich
The Wise Men were counted as wise
They could not be fooled
By the King's deceitful lies.

The gifts from the wise men
Given that night.
Foretold of the gift that God,
With all His grace and might,
Created for man, the One
That was the perfect light.
Who would removed from us
The sins of our lives.

So, when you give gifts
To those you hold dear.
Or to those not blessed
With any other holiday cheer.
Know that it is in a tradition
Started long ago,
That the gifts of peace and love
Are yours throughout the year.

A Sailor's Winter

The air is chilled
And the wind is brisk.
Its that time of year
When sailing is missed.

Instead of white sails
We see a vista of snow.
A chance for all
To watch natures great show.

But spring will return
It's just around the bend
And our season of yearning
Is soon, about to end.

ABOUT THE AUTHOR

Born in Detroit Michigan, the author is the product of a strict family environment where the expectations were, have perseverance and achieve excellence. These attributes are evidenced in his career as an engineer in the automotive industry and in his approach to his writing. A person of many interests, the author has been an avid skier, and has sailed and raced sailboats for over twenty-five years. While Mr. Papin has published several papers of a technical nature in company publications and has contributed technical information to a architectural standards book, this book of poetry is his first literary publication.

The author, now retired, resides with his family in Detroit, Michigan.

Printed in the United States
201480BV00002B/1-273/P